Search Engine Domination

**"The Ultimate Secrets to Increasing Your
Website's Visibility and Making a Ton of Cash"**

By Omar Johnson

I0469699

Table of Contents

My name is Omar Johnson and I would like to thank you for purchasing **Search Engine Domination: "The Ultimate Secrets to Increasing Your Website's Visibility and Making a Ton of Cash"**. Why such a long title? Well I guess I could of simply named this book "Search Engine Domination", but to me that title without the subtitle would of have been inappropriate and insufficient. Yes your goal should be to dominate the search engines but what would be the point of dominating the search engines if it did not lead to you making money online and profitability?

With that being said, all the valuable information contained herein is designed to give you the edge that you need to put your website at the top of the search engines and in the enviable position of being a cash generating juggernaut. Now of course whether or not you obtain that much desired goal depends on several factors which are:

1) The demand for your product or service.
2) The price of your product or service.
3) The amount of visibility your website has in the major search engines.
4) The amount of targeted traffic your website receives.

5) The ability of your website's sales copy to effectively convert prospects into paying customers.

Before I get into a detail explanation of these aforementioned factors I would presume that you are either a veteran internet marketer who is already aware and understands these factors and you have developed effective strategies in these areas and are applying them to your current online business or you are a "newbie" and totally wet behind the ears.

Nonetheless, regardless of your level of expertise the bottom line is that these factors as well as others will determine whether or not you make money online and if you are fortunate and you are already making money online, your level of mastery in these areas as well as your execution will determine how much money you actually make.

So if you are a veteran online marketer what I highly recommend is that you do not skip over any material that you think you might know because if your online business ever becomes out of whack and you are not making the sales like you use to, your troubles can always be pinpointed back to the lack of execution of the basic fundamentals.

Case in point let me give you a perfect example of this using a sports analogy. Tiger Woods the greatest golfer of our time after dominating most of his years on the professional golf tour encountered a losing streak that lasted more than two years until he won the Chevron World Challenge golf tournament. His losing streak can be traced back to several factors.

When he was winning, dominant and on top of the golf world he mastered the ability to block out all distractions and simply concentrate on the game of golf. Also his execution of the fundamentals of golf was nearly flawless. However, once he lost control of this focus and you are probably already familiar with the story which involved the revelation of many mistresses, a subsequent divorce from his wife and a bombardment of tabloid fodder, his tailspin began.

He was now unable to block out the distractions and his golf game suffered as a result because he lost his mental edge. Once he lost his mental edge and couldn't find practice time on the golf course he became rusty in the fundamentals and it translated to his inability to effectively execute to win golf tournaments. He went from being the number 1 ranked golfer in the world to being ranked number 52 and his golf earnings dropped significantly.

So what did he do to stop his slide? First he had to restore some type of order to his personal life then he had to go back to reviewing, practicing and executing the fundamentals that got him on top of the professional golf world. You have to do the same if your online business ever becomes disjointed and all of a sudden you are not experiencing the success you had before. Now let's discuss the factors.

Demand For Your Product or Services

In order to successfully sell your product or service online or anywhere else for that matter there first must be a demand for it. There is no getting around that fact. It doesn't matter what niche you are selling in. You could be selling pig slop to pot belly farmers or exquisite jewelry to high falutin divas, there still must be a demand for your product or service in order for you to make money.

Normally, you will find an existing demand for a product or service when it offers a solution to a prevailing problem. For example, there are people in the marketplace who have websites that don't have any search engine visibility and they don't know how to personally solve this particular problem so they seek out others who have that expertise as well as the solution to get them the results that they are looking for.

I give this example from personal experience because I have an SEO company GetSeoBacklinks.com (http://www.getseobacklinks.com) and my services are highly in demand because I offer to the marketplace the ultimate solution to gaining high search engine visibility and higher rankings for the keywords that are most important to them.

The majority of people actually create their product or service first without doing a proper assessment of the demand for it so they strike out more often than they hit home runs simply because they did not perform the necessary due diligence in terms of research.

So it is extremely important unless you're a wildly successful company like Apple to ascertain the pulse of the people in the niche you are intending to sell to. Identify their problems, needs, wants and fears then create services, products or a business that addresses and offers solutions to those prevailing issues and you will make money. You can get the pulse of your niche by joining and participating in related forums, discussion groups etc.

Now the way that Apple does it is quite different from what I've just mentioned. They create incredible products first and then distribute and market them to the marketplace under the premise that people don't even know yet that they actually need or want a particular Apple product like the ipod, iphone, ipad, or itunes until they have been informed about it, personally experienced it, or heard from others raving about the new gadget from Apple and how it has made their life much easier.

That was the late Steve Jobs of Apple brilliance, genius and legacy. He saw what consumers wanted even before they knew what it was. He created the demand and disrupted industries. Now I'm not saying that you can't create the demand like Apple does, hey you just might be on that path but what I am saying is that regardless of your strategy there must be a demand for what you are offering to the marketplace. When you have determined that there is indeed a demand for your product or service, your marketing message must make that connection to the audience you are trying to attract. Once you have successfully reeled them in, you must deliver value.

The Price of Your Product or Service

When deciding what price to affix to a product or service many online marketers experience self doubt. There is an annoying back and forth conflicting internal conversation that occurs between the ears questioning whether or not they are charging too much or too little for the product or service that they are offering.

But does the price of a product or service really matter? Sure it does on many accounts. Let me explain. If you are selling a product or service and you haven't differentiated it from the many others that are selling that same exact product or service you are selling then it's a commodity. It is a commodity because there is nothing unique about it. It's generic. So people decide to buy it or not solely based on the price.

For instance take a generic product like a screwdriver. Every hardware and convenience store are selling them in your local area. It is a commoditized product. So if you walk into a store that is selling a screwdriver for $10, would you buy it when you know that every other store in your local area is selling the same exact screwdriver for $2? Of course you wouldn't.

Well the same concept applies to selling online. If you are a selling a commoditized product or service people will make their decision to buy from you based on price. The problem with that is there is always someone who is willing to sell what you are selling cheaper. So where does that leave you? In my estimation it puts you and your online business in a very vulnerable position.

You're vulnerable because your competitors will slash their prices to compete with you with little regard to how it will even affect their profits. Since consumers are price conscious when it comes to commoditized products or services you have no choice but to slash your prices to match your competition. This price slashing spiral goes on and on until you can't do it any longer, throw in the towel or eventually go out of business. Not a pretty sight!

Personally, I don't engage in selling commodity type products or services simply because I know the end result. Now I'm not saying I don't sell products or services that have some similarity to what others are selling, but I'm smart enough to differentiate and distinguish my offerings to make them unique and one of a kind. You should do the same. How? By creating a unique selling proposition (USP).

Unique Selling Proposition (USP)

A unique selling proposition is what sets your products or services apart from your competitors. It is a statement, concept, idea or a way of doing business that tells your potential customers why they should do business with you over someone else. Federal Express is a perfect example of what a strong USP can do for your business.

When Fred Smith founded Federal Express he filled a void because during that time there was no such thing as an air freight company that delivered your package overnight and on time. When you sent your package through other companies like the United States Postal Service, you could only hope that your package got to its destination in a reasonable time. Essentially you had no peace of mind.

Federal Express brilliantly capitalized on what was missing in the marketplace by offering a delivery service that absolutely guaranteed that your package would get to its destination overnight. They immediately distinguished themselves from their competitors by creating one of the greatest unique selling propositions of all time.

"When your package absolutely, positively has to get there overnight"

Federal Express trumpeted this USP over and over again in its advertising and propelled itself into an international multibillion dollar business. Their prices were higher than other delivery services, but it did not matter to their customers because not only were they offering something rare and unique, they were also giving their customers a peace of mind. So the lesson here is that your customers will pay premium prices if what you are offering is unique, fills a void and gives them a peace of mind and satisfaction. Here are some other notable examples of strong USPs.

Domino's Pizza

"You get fresh, hot pizza delivered to your door in 30 minutes or less or it's free"

M&Ms

"The milk chocolate melts in your mouth, not in your hand"

DeBeers

"Diamonds are forever"

Avis

"We're number two. We try harder"

Wheaties

"The breakfast of champions"

Barnum and Bailey Circus

"The greatest show on earth"

Gatorade

"The thirst quencher"

Bounty Paper Towels

"The quicker picker upper"

Gillette

"The best a man can get"

Creating a USP For Your Product Or Service

As an online entrepreneur it is imperative that you price your products and services adequately enough to make a profit and stay in business because if you don't it will result in the death of your business. Even better, the pricing of your product or services should actually put you in the position to thrive financially not just stay in business because just "staying in business" is a path of mediocrity and you're better than that.

Conversely, if you're doing your online business without the aid of a 9 to 5 job, the income you generate must pay for your food, clothing, rent or mortgage, utilities, transportation and other essentials as well as your business expenses. That is the pull no punches reality of your situation. So pricing is super important which means you must be systematic in your approach to it.

The way that you can be systematic in your approach is by deciding what to sell and how to sell it so that you don't become a victim of the commodity price slashing competition that I mentioned previously.

When deciding what to sell and how to sell it this is what I strongly suggest. You should either create your own proprietary product or service or add a proprietary aspect to an existing product or service or do both. Once you have decided on the direction you are going to take you must then craft a strong USP that communicates to the marketplace the benefit, value and uniqueness of your product or service.

There is a step by step process that I use to create a USP for my products and services and I would like to share it with you so that you can use it as a blueprint when creating yours.

Step 1: Know Your Niche or Industry

It is essential that you thoroughly understand the niche or industry that you are targeting. This is simply accomplished by doing research. For example, if your goal was to sell fishing rods online to fishermen who specialize in catching bass fish you should be knowledgeable about the different types of fishing rods that presently exist in the marketplace for bass fishermen.

Not only must you be knowledgeable about bass fishing rods, but you have to be familiar with the jargon, the demographics and psychographics of bass fishermen, the various challenges and concerns that they face when bass fishing like trying to find the right bait or whether to use a fiberglass or graphite fishing rod.

This will enable you to create a customer profile which will help you make better decisions about how to spend your marketing dollars and minimize the mistakes caused by not knowing your customer base.

Step 2: Understand The Needs And Wants Of The Marketplace

When you understand the needs and wants of your customer base and deliver the products or services that satisfy those particular needs and wants, you will make sales if the message in your marketing makes an emotional connection and resonates with your niche.

So find out what kind of service or product that your customer base is pining for or just ask them. I know that sounds simple, but sometimes to find out what people actually want you have to ask them. I do this all the time with my customers by giving them surveys and questionnaires that are designed to find out what they want in terms of a product or service. Once I get their feedback I look for the commonalities in their answers then I proceed to create that killer product or service that satisfies them.

Step 3: Analyze And Understand Your Competition

Before you can create your unique selling proposition, you need to analyze and understand your competition. Start your competitor analysis by identifying the leading companies in your niche or industry. The internet often makes this easy to do, but what if you can't seem to find any major competitors just by searching through Google?

You might need to pick up a phone book and take a look at the ads, or search through back issues of local business journals if your competitors are based locally.

If your competitors are all over the U.S. or international, then you will have to be a little more creative. Look at advertisements on major websites, listing in directories, etc. Once you have the leaders pinpointed, map out what you know about them. Specifically, analyze the product or service that you will be competing with. Dissect its strengths and weaknesses.

Step 4: Determine or Create Your Uniqueness

Now that you have the facts and information about your competitors product or service compare it to yours. Determine what separates your product or service from theirs. Are there any unique features or benefits that you offer and they don't? Do you offer any bonuses? Do you offer free shipping?

If you can't find something that is uniquely special about your product or service that distinguishes it from your competition then you must add something to it that does. This will enable you to create a strong USP.

Step 5: Create A Killer USP

Once you have conquered steps 1-4 you can now begin to create that killer USP for your product or service. Keep in mind that your USP should be very simple; one sentence or a statement that is believable and that clearly illustrates a unique benefit that a customer will get from your product. "Buy this product, and you will get this specific benefit."

Your USP should also highlight something that your competition doesn't offer and ideally it should be difficult for them to copy. Let me give you a demonstration of the thought process and the aforementioned steps I went through to create a killer USP for my lead generation software called "The GMap Lead Generator". By the way I offer a 2 day free trial for this software and you can sign up here:

http://www.gmapleadgenerator.com/freetrial.html

First of all I must admit that I initially created "The GMap Lead Generator" based on my own personal wants and needs. I run multiple businesses both online and offline and as such with any business regardless of the niche you must be able to consistently generate leads because they are the lifeblood of a business. Leads turn into prospects and prospects convert into sales and sales equals money in the bank.

Now the way I previously went about obtaining leads before I created "The GMap Lead Generator" was I would spend money buying lists from list brokers. Sometimes those lists worked well and sometimes they didn't. What I really detested was that each time I needed a list of leads I had to pay a minimum of $500 which was the list broker's requirement and is standard in the mailing list industry. Needless to say I was burning a hole in my pockets.

I even subscribed to a database service with a company named Brad & Dunstreet to obtain leads which also cost me a small fortune. I was actually paying about $700 per month to use this service.

Frustrated with those costs associated with obtaining leads I had a strong desire and a need to drastically reduce those expenses or eliminate them totally. So I decided to create "The GMap Lead Generator" which is an automated lead generation software that allows me to obtain business leads via the internet at virtually no cost.

This software worked so well for me that I surmised that it would work for others as well. So what I did was embark on a research campaign to find out about the lead generation niche, the various software that existed in the marketplace and the type of people who would be ideal candidates to use this specific lead generation tool. As a result of my research, I concluded that there was indeed a need for a tool like the GMap Lead Generator but before releasing it to the public I wanted to enhance it further so that it completely filled the void in the marketplace. I perused the forums and chat rooms to learn what people actually wanted and needed in a lead generation software and simply incorporated it.

During this time, I also analyzed and dissected the other companies in the marketplace that were also selling lead generation software. I mapped out their strengths and weaknesses and what made my product uniquely different from theirs. I then added more relevant features to the GMap Lead Generator to make it even more unique.

Once I was done with the finishing touches I created a killer USP that highlighted the benefits of the software and what uniquely separated it from the competition and released it to the marketplace. Here is that killer USP I created.

"The Set It And Forget Software That Automatically Finds And Collects For You All The Local Business Leads You Can Handle In <u>Any Niche</u> In 4 Different Countries Using The Google Maps System"

So in essence, this strong USP along with the benefits and uniqueness of the product enabled me to price it at whatever price that I deemed as appropriate rather than being dictated by my competitors pricing.

The Amount of Visibility Your Website Has In The Major Search Engines

As an online entrepreneur it is essential that your website has high visibility in the 3 major search engines Google, Yahoo and Bing because when people are looking for a product or service that will help them solve a particular problem the majority of the time they use the search engines.

So if your website is nowhere to be found how would they ever be able to discover you? This is why serious online entrepreneurs will do everything in their power and fight tooth and nail to get high rankings for the keywords that are most important to their website because where you are ranked will determine how much relevant targeted organic traffic you will receive at your website.

The more relevant targeted traffic you receive the more money you will make if your product or service is commercially viable, in demand and your conversion rate is high. Let me share with you some vital statistics that hammers home this point.

- 85% of Internet users find websites through search engines.
- 98% of people searching for something online never go past the first page of search results.
- A number 1 ranking = 42% of the search engine traffic.
- A number 2 ranking = 12% of the search engine traffic.
- A number 3 ranking = 9% of the search engine traffic.

As you can clearly see the further down you are in the rankings the percentage of clicks a website gets decreases. Since 98% of consumers don't go past page one when doing searches, you at least want to be on page one and ideally it would be great to get that number 1 ranking!

Pay Per Click Advertising

Organic (natural) search results are not the only way for your website to obtain search engine visibility. You can also utilize pay per click advertising. The most notable pay per click advertising program is Google Adwords. There is also the Microsoft Advertising Ad Center platform which incorporates both Bing and Yahoo search engines.

I don't want to jump the gun and assume that you know how pay per click advertising works so let me briefly explain it. Pay per click or PPC is a method for generating traffic wherein you pay for every visitor that goes to your website by clicking on your advertising link.

The cost that you pay per click is determined by the original bid that you placed on the particular keyword that resulted in your ad being shown in the search engines. So if you bid let's say 60 cents for the keyword "Dog Trainer" and someone clicked on your ad it will cost you 60 cents or less depending on what others have bid for that exact keyword, your quality score and your click through rate when advertising on Google Adwords.

Pay per click advertising is a big part of my search engine domination strategy. I use it mainly because it is effective, I am able to get immediate results and it represents 15% of all search engine traffic on the internet. Conversely, organic (natural) search results listings receive 85% of all search engine clicks.

So if your ultimate goal is to dominate the search engines, I highly suggest that you employ both strategies, getting your website to rank high in the organic search results and pay per click advertising only if it works for you, is proven to be effective and you can get an acceptable return on your investment.

When investing in pay per click advertising you must use good economic common sense in determining whether it is working for you. The ultimate guideline for any pay per click advertising is how much business is it bringing you? If you're paying $100 per day in click fees to advertise cell phones, but you're only generating $75 per day in revenue from that ad then you either need to cut back on your advertising (lowering your per click bids) or improve your site's conversion rate from visitor to sale.

It's important not to get too attached to ads that don't work just because you think they should work. It may take as little as a week, or as long as three months to determine whether a particular pay per click ad is effective, but as long as you monitor your spending and your earnings closely and adjust your ads accordingly, you can generate positive income with paid search listings.

Other advantages of pay per click advertising

- You get immediate results. Google Adwords ads become live in their search engine within 10 minutes of the ad being placed.
- Your website receives targeted relevant traffic from the search engines as well as from partner websites that participate in the affiliate programs like Google Adsense.
- You only spend what your budget allows.

Dominating The Search Engines Through SEO Article Writing And Article Directory Submission

Another strategy that I use without fail to make my websites highly visible in the search engines is by writing SEO articles and submitting them to the many thousands of article directories that are on the internet. An SEO article is simply an article that is written specifically to contain a repeated fair usage of your main keywords or keyword phrases with the purpose of getting targeted search engine traffic and gaining higher search engine rankings for your website.

SEO is an acronym for search engine optimization. I give a detailed explanation of what SEO is later on in this book if you don't fully understand it at this point.

Now the way that you would use article writing and article directory submission to dominate the search engines is that article directories allow you to include at the end of each article you have written an author's resource box. This resource box can contain a brief description of your product or service and your website's link.

This is golden to you in your quest for search engine domination. Here's why. Your articles based on my personal experience which includes writing articles for myself and my many clients will get indexed and appear in the search engines if they get done and optimized the right way.

Some of them will even attain high search engine rankings giving your website instant search engine visibility indirectly through the author's resource box where you would put your product or service description and a link that goes directly back to your website.

Brilliant right? Obviously there is more than one way to skin a cat and obtain your goal of search engine domination. By the way, since the author's resource box is one of the main reasons for the creation of your article (another main reason is to provide valuable information to your potential customers so that they will make an emotional connection to you) shouldn't it be crafted in a way that is going to yield the best results?

The author's resource box is your only chance to convert your article readers into leads and sales for your online business. Like I previously mentioned to you in the opening paragraph of this book "What would be the point of dominating the search engines if it did not lead to you making money online and profitability?"

The first sentence in your author's resource box should introduce you or your business to the reader. After all, your readers can't do business with someone they don't know. After that you need to create a strong "call to action" something that inspires and motivates your readers to click on your website's link in the resource box.

What I normally do as an enticement is offer something free that that the reader can subscribe to like a free e-course, newsletter or special report, to get them further exposed to my expertise. Here is an actual "call to action" that I presently use in my article's resource box to entice readers to visit my GetSeoBacklinks.com website:

"Learn the secrets of getting your website on the first page of Google, Yahoo and Bing with our FREE e-course entitled "Powerful Tips That Will Enable Your Website To Rank High On The Search Engines" visit http://www.getseobacklinks.com.

I must note that another important thing that you gain from SEO article writing and submission to the many article directories are backlinks to your website which are one of the main variables that affect how high your website ranks in the search engines. I will also give you a detailed explanation on backlinks and how they work to determine your website's ranking shortly.

Now let me give you a vivid example of how the combined prowess of SEO article writing and article directory submission, pay per click advertising and ranking high through organic search results allowed me to dominate the first page of Google for the keyword phrases "How to create a land trust", "How to form a land trust", and "How to operate a land trust" for my site http://www.createalandtrust.com where I sell a home study course on how to protect real estate by use of a land trust.

First I created a domain name (createalandtrust.com) to match one of the keyword phrases ("create a land trust") that I wanted to rank high for in the search engines. Then I created a killer keyword enriched sales letter that served as the foundation for my one page mini-site. I wrote my sales letter using a technique referred to as SEO copywriting.

SEO copywriting is the technique of writing the viewable text on a web page in such a way that it reads well for your website's visitors and also targets specific search terms. Its intended purpose is to rank high in the search engines for those targeted search terms.

So when you are writing the text for your website, mini-site, affiliate page or blog it has to be written in a scientific way. This includes having the proper keyword density, keyword frequency, keyword prominence and keyword proximity. Let me explain these concepts.

Keyword density – is the percentage of times a keyword or keyword phrase appears on a web page compared to the total number of words on the page. The preferred keyword density ratio varies from search engine to search engine. What I normally use for my websites like the createalandtrust.com site we are discussing is a keyword density ratio of 3-9%.

Keyword frequency – Keyword frequency refers to the number of times a keyword or keyword phrase appears within a web page. In SEO, the theory is that the more times a keyword or keyword phrase appears within a web page, the more relevance a search engine is likely to give the page for a search containing those keywords.

A word of caution, you don't want to abuse and unnecessarily repeat your keywords or keyword phrases over and over again because this is considered by the search engines to be "keyword stuffing" and your website will be penalized for it.

Keyword prominence – refers to the prominent placement of keywords or keyword phrases within a web page. Prominent placement may be in the page header, meta tags, opening paragraph, or at the start of a sentence.

Keyword proximity – Keyword proximity refers to the closeness between two or more keywords. The closer the keywords are the better it is for the search rankings. For example, the name of my course is **"How To Form and Operate Land Trusts"**. It also happens to be another one of the keyword phrases I wanted to rank high for so it is prominently placed throughout my website. In addition, it is also included in the title bar of my web page.

When people are searching for information on how to create a land trust they will usually type in one of the following search queries: "How to form a land trust", "How to operate a land trust" and "How to create a land trust" so I made sure that my website's keyword proximity matched exactly the order in which they were typing these keywords in the search engines because it impacts the rankings.

For instance, the keyword phrase "How to form a land trust" is likely to rank higher in the search engines than the keyword phrase "How a land trust is formed" when a person types in the search query "How to form a land trust" because of the keyword proximity. I say "likely" because there are also other factors that are involved in determining where a website will rank in the search engines.

After I completed this on page optimization of my website, I created some powerful backlinks to it which eventually enabled me to obtain a number one ranking in the organic search results on Google, Yahoo and Bing for the aforementioned keyword phrases.

During that same period I also wrote 10 different SEO articles on land trusts and submitted them to the many article directories online. I also created powerful backlinks to these articles and as a result two of them ended up occupying the 3rd and 5th position on the first page of Google.

To top it all off, I created a Google Adwords, Yahoo Search and Microsoft Ad center pay per click advertisement that landed me on the first page of those respective search engines for those same keyword phrases. I completely and methodically dominated the major search engines and it translated into a boatload of sales.

The Amount of Targeted Traffic Your Website Receives

The amount of <u>targeted traffic</u> your website receives is one of the main factors that will determine if you're going to succeed online. Some people get fooled into thinking that any type of traffic will do as long as they receive visitors to their website. This is erroneous thinking because the traffic that you receive that is not targeted from the niche you are trying to attract will have zero impact on your site in terms of generating sales and the overall level of interest.

You want the people that visit your site to have an interest in what your site is about. If you're selling products or services you want them to have an interest in those products or services so that you can make sales.

If you're an affiliate and the way that you make your money is by people clicking on the ads that populate your site they at least have to be interested in your site so that they can stay on long enough to click on something.

So targeted traffic is key and is what you should be aiming for. In fact, your overall marketing strategy should be primarily designed to get a lot of targeted traffic to your site. To determine the type of traffic and the amount of visitors you are getting at your website and whether these visitors are converting to leads or sales you need to measure everything that goes on at your website. The way that I measure performance at my various websites is by using a free tracking tool offered by Google called Google Analytics.

The Power Of Google Analytics

Once you have installed the tracking code on your website, Google Analytics begins to generate detailed statistics about the visitors and web traffic that you receive. Google Analytics keeps track of all visitors to your website, the particular country that they came from, how they arrived, where they landed at, how long they stayed and the exact keywords that they typed into the search engines to get to your site.

In addition, Google Analytics tracks referred visitors sent by other websites that link to you and you can also set up your account to track all conversions on your website as well as the conversions that result from your Google Adwords pay per click campaigns.

Measuring your website's metrics is the only way that you will truly be able to understand what's working or not working on your website and the overall effectiveness of your marketing and advertising campaigns. These are the following metrics you should be paying close attention to.

1) How many visitors your website is receiving and how many of those visitors are converting to customers.

This is referred to as your visitor to customer conversion rate and it is a measurement of how effectively you are convincing buyers to buy from you. The formula is as follows:

# of sales / # of visitors X 100 = Visitor to customer conversion rate

So if you received a total of 5,000 visits for the month at your website and 170 became customers then your visitor to customer conversion rate is 3.4%. To improve upon your visitor to customer conversion rate you may want to tweak your website sales copy a little by perhaps turning your ordinary offers into irresistible ones or by increasing the amount of visitors to your site or a combination of both.

2) Bounce Rate

The bounce rate is the number of people who come to a page of your site, and then leave without clicking anything else. A high bounce rate may be indicative of not attracting the right audience to your website or it might be a strong indication that your website content is not "sticky" enough.

3) Traffic Sources

The source of your traffic is another extremely important metric. Google Analytics shows you where the traffic you received at your site originated from. You get a complete percentage breakdown in a pie chart graph. The breakdown is as follows: The percentage of visitors from search traffic, the percentage of visitors from referral traffic and the percentage of visitors from direct traffic which are the people who visited your website by typing in the actual url.

In my opinion, having a healthy balance of search, referral and direct traffic is essential for the stability of your online business. You protect yourself from becoming victimized by having an over reliance on one form of traffic. For example, if you strictly relied on traffic from the search engines and Google makes an algorithm change like they did with the Panda update that results in a precipitous drop in the rankings for your website, it will have a dramatic impact on your earnings.

4) Entrance Keywords

This metric tells you what keywords or keyword phrases are driving traffic to your website from the search engines. This is important to know because if your website visitors are finding your site with keywords that don't match your intended target you will have a problem with your conversions. If you encounter this problem, to correct it all you would have to simply do is optimize your website to reflect the proper keyword usage.

5) Time on Page

Knowing the amount of time that each visitor is spending on specific web pages on my site is valuable information that I use to determine the effectiveness and the "stickiness" of my content. Obviously the higher time a visitor spends on a particular web page, the better the content I am creating and the lower time that they spend means I need to ramp up my content.

6) Landing Page

Your website's visitors will not always land on the entrance page of your website. The entrance page is basically the web page that they land on when they type in your domain name. They will also land on other pages within your website and you need to know where they are landing so that you are able to achieve optimal results from those specific landing pages.

The Ability Of Your Website's Sales Copy To Effectively Convert Prospects Into Paying Customers

Most often times when a website is getting a fair amount of targeted traffic but is not receiving a decent amount of sales in spite of having a good product or service, the problem can usually be traced to ineffective sales copy that doesn't inspire or persuade visitors to buy.

So when you are writing sales copy for your products or services make sure that it persuasively communicates and conveys to your potential customers "What's in it for them?" when they purchase your product or service.

You do this by enthusiastically highlighting the benefits and the value that they will receive.

The reason why I say that you must do it enthusiastically is because when was the last time you bought something from an unenthusiastic sales person? Personally, I can't recall ever doing so. Well having sales copy on your website that lacks enthusiasm and doesn't inspire will have that same effect.

To assist you in improving your website's sales copy and conversion rate the following is a list of "Words That Sell" that you can utilize.

Words That Convey Value

• Accepted

• Acclaimed

• Admired

• Approved

• Authorized

• Certified

• Commended

• Complimented

- Endorsed

- Guaranteed

- Honored

- Lauded

- Popular

- Praised

- Proven

- Recognized

- Recommended

- Sanctioned

- Tested

Words That Convey Quality

- Authentic

- Better

- Choice

- Durable

- Excellent

- Exclusive

- Famous

- Fine

- First-Rate

- Genuine

- Good

- Greatest

- Imported

- Improved

- Limited

- Noted

- Outstanding

- Personalized

- Rare

- Remarkable

- Rugged

- Selected

- Special

- Superior

- Surpassing

- Terrific

- Top

- Unique

- Unparalleled

- Unsurpassed

- Valuable

- Wonderful

Words That Convey Surprise

- Amazing

- Astonishing

- Astounding

- Exceptional

- Extraordinary

- Fantastic

- Magic

- Miracle

- Notable

- Noteworthy

- Remarkable

- Sensational

The Irresistible Offer

In addition to having stellar sales copy if you want to really explode your sales and fatten your bank account with your online business you need to make the offers on your products or services irresistible. What is an irresistible offer? An irresistible offer is one that overwhelms your prospects with value so much that it becomes a total no brainer for them to part with their money.

For example online shoe giant Zappos.com irresistible offer to its customers is that it has a two-way free shipping policy. Zappos ships your shoes for free and if you don't like them not only will they refund your money but they also pay to pick the shoes up. What's even more amazing is that they have a 365 day return policy.

How successful has this irresistible offer been for them? They sell over a billion dollars in shoes annually!

Here are some of the things that you can do to make your offers irresistible:

- **Create a powerful risk reversal** - Risk reversal is when the seller assumes the risk for a purchase instead of a buyer. Normally when you buy something there is some risk associated with it. Perhaps you don't like it, it is not the right size or color, it doesn't perform the way you would like etc.

  What this does is create a psychological barrier or hurdle that prevents a purchase from occurring. The way that you would eliminate this hurdle is by reversing the risk which entails shifting the risk from the customer to you. The way that you would shift the risk is by offering a strong no questions asked money back guarantee that gives the customer the confidence to purchase from you.

  Here is the strong money back guarantee that I use to eliminate the risk for my customers when they purchase my land trust course that I referred to previously:

"Your satisfaction is important to me, and I personally guarantee it when you order "How To Form And Operate Land Trusts" with my no risk, you-can't-lose, 100%, no-questions-asked, iron-clad money back guarantee. If for any reason you aren't thrilled and satisfied with my product, just contact me within 30 days and I'll refund 100% of your purchase price. No hard feelings."

- **Offer Your Customers a FREE "Test Drive"** – You probably wouldn't buy a car without test driving it first. By the same accord, whenever appropriate how can you expect someone to buy your product or service without trying it? By letting your customers "try it before they buy it" you convey that you have confidence and believe in your product or service.

   It also shows that you care about your customers because you want to make sure they're a good fit before they buy. Use this "test drive" strategy and watch your conversions rates skyrocket and your refund rate drop to practically zero.

- **Add Premium Bonuses** – Adding high quality, relevant, premium bonuses can boost the perceived value of your product or service sky high. If possible, the value of the bonus should come close to the actual price of the main product. That way, your customers will feel as if they have gotten a great bargain. In fact, in many cases a customer will purchase because they want the bonuses and not necessarily the main product.

How To Use A/B Split Testing To Increase Conversions

The way that you can increase the conversions on your website is by using A/B split testing. A/B split testing is the process of testing the conversion capability of one sales page versus another. For example, if you had two possible headlines for your webpage but couldn't decide which one to use or which one will yield the best results, you could run an A/B split test in which half of your visitors would see Headline A and the other half would see Headline B.

Then you would calculate the conversion rate for each headline to determine which headline produced the best results. Not only can you use A/B split testing to determine which headline to use but you can also test other page elements such as subheads, bulleted points, text, images and prices. You can test these elements individually or all at once.

When you are testing all the variables at the same time this is called "multivariate testing". Google offers a free tool called the "Google Website Optimizer" that allows you to perform both A/B split and multivariate testing.

Don't Let Your Visitors Get Away And Leave Money On The Table

The most common mistake that online businesses make is not having something on their website that will enable them to capture the names, email addresses, telephone numbers and other vital information of their many visitors. It is a known fact that the majority of the people who visit a website don't buy on the initial visit. The buying usually happens after they had multiple correspondences from you.

So it is very important that you have the ability to follow up with your visitors so that they can become more acquainted with your company and the products or services that you are offering. If you don't have the ability to follow up with them then essentially you are leaving money on the table.

The easiest way to capture your visitor's information and also automatically follow up with them in a sequential fashion at different intervals is by using an autoresponder. You would entice your visitors to "opt in" and sign up to receive messages from you by offering something of value like a free report, audio, newsletter, e-course etc. The autoresponder service that I presently use on all my websites is called AWeber.

AWeber allows you to track various statistics in your email marketing campaigns like who opened your email and who didn't, which links were clicked on and by whom, how much revenue your message generated and how many people subscribed or unsubscribed.

The important lesson here is, if you are going to dominate the search engines and receive a great deal of traffic for doing so then you need to make sure that your website has the appropriate lead capturing tool so you can through a series of correspondences make a connection with your visitors and convert them from prospects into paying customers.

Now that we thoroughly covered the main factors that will determine whether your website will be a cash generating juggernaut let's move on with a detail explanation of SEO.

Search Engine Optimization (SEO)

SEO is the process and science of making sure that a website remains relevant to the search engines by ranking high for its main keywords and keyword phrases.

This process includes on-page optimization and off-page optimization.

On-page optimization is simply working directly on the elements on your website to get it to rank high on the search engines and off-page optimization is everything that you do off your website to get it to rank high on the search engines.

Let's review the factors that are involved in on page and off page optimization:

On-Page Optimization Factors

- **Keyword Research, Analysis and Implementation** – Keyword research then coming to the appropriate decision as to what are the best possible keywords to implement on your website so that you will attract targeted visitors and be found in the search engines is the most crucial part of the SEO process for obvious reasons. Get it right and you will see major results, get it wrong and it will be a waste of your time, money and energy.

  You can do keyword research by using the Google Keyword Tool. Simply enter your main keywords into the tool and review the results.

The results will show you a 12 month average of what keywords and keyword variations people are using in their search queries on Google. Google's keyword tool gives you a nice breakdown by showing you the average monthly global and local searches that have occurred and the level of competition for those keywords if you decided to advertise using Google Adwords.

If you are located in the United States, the local searches represent the monthly average searches that occurred in the United States and the global searches represent the monthly average searches that occurred worldwide. If you live in another country, the Google keyword tool automatically defaults to your country and the local searches will represent all the searches that occurred in your country and the global searches will remain the same and represent worldwide searches.

Let me show you a vivid example of how you would use the Google keyword tool to obtain your keywords if you were creating a website in the "dog training" niche. Where it says word or phrase you would type in the keywords "dog training" and then click on the search button to render the results. The following is a partial list of those results.

Keyword	Competition	Global Searches	Local Searches
Dog training	Medium	1,500,000	823,000
Dog training schools	High	49,500	22,200
Dog obedience training	High	110,000	49,500
Dog training advice	Low	3,600	2,400
Free dog training	High	8,100	5.400
Dog training tips	Medium	22,200	12,100
Online dog training	High	6,600	4,400
Dog training courses	High	90,500	33,100
Dog training obedience	High	110,000	49,500

It is obvious from reading these results that the dog training niche is a very popular one because of the many searches done locally and globally. Specifically, the keyword "Dog Training" has a combined search total of 2,323,000 so of course you would have to make sure you have the proper keyword density and keyword prominence with this particular keyword to put your website in the position to capitalize on some of this traffic.

Primarily, what I do before I construct a website is use the keyword tool to determine what are the most frequent search queries in a particular niche and then I build an online business around them. For example, based on this particular search we are analyzing I would focus on the micro-niche "dog obedience training" and probably offer dog obedience training home study courses and other related materials for sale on my website.

Don't forget about your long tail keyword strategy - Long tail keywords are keyword phrases composed of three or more words that collectively are more specific than a single keyword. In general, long tail keywords are more likely to convert to sales because they are more buyer specific and there is less competition for them. For example, "Power drill" is a keyword and Black & Decker HPD18AK-2 18-Volt Power Drill is the targeted long tail version.

The two best ways to come up with long tail keywords for your website:

1) **Think from a customer's perspective**. What would you typically type in the search engines to find a particular product or website if you were the customer? Just

simply use a common sense approach and you will come up with answers that will enable you to come up with the long tail keywords for your site.

2) **Use the** Keyword Labs Question Tool **from Wordtracker** – The Keyword Labs Question Tool is a free tool that allows you to bring back the relevant questions people are asking in relation to any given keyword. For example, here are some of the questions that are returned for the keyword "dog obedience training".

How old should your dog be when you start obedience training?

How early can dog obedience training begin?

What is a good age to begin obedience training for a dog?

- **Title Tag** - Your website's title tag is a very important on page optimization element because it shows up in the search engine results as a clickable headline. So when you are creating your title tags for your various web pages make sure you come up with the most relevant title in relationship to your keywords and the content on your web page.

Your title tag should be descriptive, short and appealing. It should also include your main keywords in which you would like to rank for. It is best to put your keywords first in your title and when possible use modifiers because people tend to include them in their search. Modifiers are words like "cheap", "best", "premium", "buy".

- **Meta Tags** - Meta tags are HTML codes that are inserted into the header on a web page, after the title tag. Meta tags are not viewable by your website's visitors. Here is the HTML syntax for meta tags.

  <META NAME="Description" CONTENT="Your descriptive sentence or two goes here.">

  Although search engines have shifted away in their emphasis on meta tags I still like to use them.

- **Heading or H Tags** - Headings are pieces of html code that allow you to make certain words stand out on a web page. The most important heading tags to search engines are H1 tags. The H1 tag is the highest level tag that guides search engine crawlers to the most relevant words on a web page. There are six types of header tags that range from H1 to H6. Here are examples.

<h1>Heading</h1>

<h2>Heading</h2>

<h3>Heading</h3>

<h4>Heading</h4>

<h5>Heading</h5>

<h6>Heading</h6>

It is imperative that you use your header tags in a logical way with the appropriate structure. Your H1 tag should be at the top of the page of your content and theoretically you shouldn't use it more than once. You should follow a hierarchical structure with the H1 tag first followed by the H2, H3, H4, H5, and H6 tags.

- **Alt tags** – An ALT tag is alternative text that is displayed within an image tag. Your Alt tag description would help visitors to your site visualize the images that they can't see as a result of maybe the browser not loading the image properly or perhaps they are visually impaired and are using a screen reader. You should use an alt tag on all your images because not only does it help your visitors gain accessibility but it also helps the search engines decipher what your site is about because they are unable to see images.

Here is an example of an alt tag:

<img src="image1.jpg" alt="This is a dog trainer teaching a dog obedience">

- **Internal link structure** – Internal link structure refers to all the links within your website. The search engines evaluate the hierarchy of your internal links. They look at what pages are linked together and which pages are not. This is important because links = votes.

  For example, let's say you have two pages on your website Page A and Page B and you have Page A linking via anchor text to Page B because they are relevant to each other in terms of keywords and content. Page A is viewed by the search engines as essentially voting for Page B in regards to its overall keyword relevancy and content. The more votes Page B gets the better chance it will have to rank for its keywords.

It is also important that you make sure that your site doesn't have any broken links and you are using keyword rich anchor texts. An anchor text is the visible clickable text in a hyperlink. The words contained in the text usually your keywords will determine the ranking that a page will get in the search engines.

Here is an example of how an anchor text would look:

Premium Backlinks

This anchor text example contains the keywords "Premium Backlinks" which is relevant to my website GetSeoBacklinks.com. When you click on it, you automatically go to the site.

- **Submission of XML Sitemap** – Creating and submitting an XML Sitemap is a very essential part of the on-page optimization process. A XML Sitemap is basically a map of your site that tells the search engine or anyone else that is viewing your Sitemap where to search providing them with urls to follow. A XML Sitemap lists all of your site's urls and this enables search engine spiders to crawl and index your site. This is extremely important because some pages on your site may not be discoverable through the normal search engine crawling process.

Backlinks

Now that we have covered the on-page optimization factors let's discuss the off page optimization factors. Off page optimization is all about link building and backlinks. Backlinks also referred to as inbound links are basically links that are directed towards your website.

The number of quality backlinks that your site has is an indication to the search engines of the popularity or importance of your website and is used to determine where your site will rank. Backlinks are also hugely important because they bring traffic to your website.

So how do you determine what a quality backlink is? Most people would say it's strictly based on page rank. The assumption is the higher the page rank of the site you are getting the backlink from the better the quality that backlink is and the lower the page rank means there is a drop off in quality. I wholeheartedly disagree with this assumption and I define a quality backlink as any backlink that helps your site improve its ranking in the search engines because isn't that the aim?

In case you didn't know what a page rank is let me explain. A page rank is a link analysis algorithm that was created by and named after Larry Page one of the co-founders of Google. What this algorithm does is assign a value to each web page on the internet with the intended purpose of being able to rank these web pages in relation to each other.

Page rank values range from 0 (pr0) to 10 (pr10), with 10 being the highest. The values assigned signify the level of importance of a site to Google.

Here are a few popular sites that have a page rank of 10 (pr10):

Yahoo.com
DMOZ.com
Microsoft.com
Apple.com
UsaToday.com
Adobe.com
Nasa.gov
Mit.edu

Returning back to our discussion of what a quality backlink is. Many website owners misunderstand the concept of link building and engage in strategies that can adversely affect their website's ranking.

For example, if they have a new website (0-4 months old) they erroneous think that the quicker they can obtain a ton of high pr value backlinks to their site the sooner they will rank high in the search engines. So they only focus on obtaining a certain range of high pr backlinks. For instance, only backlinks with a pr value of 5 -7 not understanding that this will arouse the suspicion of the search engines because normally this is not considered to be a natural progression for a new website.

Think about what I said for a moment. A new website out the gate doesn't normally receive a slew of high pr backlinks with a pr ranging from 5-7. Usually, a new site will get backlinks from sites with pr values of 0-3 then over a course of time they will obtain high pr backlinks as their site becomes more known and more popular. This natural progression is of course not etched in stone and is not always the case, but you must always remember that search engines are on the lookout for websites that try to "in their eyes" artificially manipulate their rankings.

To remain out of the cross hairs of the search engines don't leave what we call in the SEO world bad "footprints" when doing your link building. Leaving bad "footprints" as it relates to backlinks are identifiable suspicious patterns that you leave behind that can be easily detected by the search engines. So if you're a new website and you are only obtaining backlinks from pr 5-7 websites, this is easily detectable by the search engines and it might result in you being punished in the search rankings or may land your website in what is known as the Google "Sandbox".

The Google "Sandbox" is sort of a purgatory for websites who land in Google's cross hairs. What happens to a site that unfortunately lands in the "Sandbox" is that they are no longer listed in Google's search engine. The "Sandbox" is not necessarily a permanent thing, but to get out of it you have to be skilled enough to set your website on the right course. So the key is don't do things that will land you there in the first place!

Conversely, another common mistake that new website owners make is that they create a ton of backlinks too fast without first aging their domain. Most of the time they are victimized by these fly by night SEO companies on the internet who are offering to build 10,000 – 50,000 backlinks in one day for $10.

After they purchase these types of backlink packages and their website becomes predictably and adversely affected, they wonder "why have my search engine rankings dropped? or "why is my website not listed in

Google?" I can practically guarantee to you that the people who buy these packages don't know about the Google "Sandbox" like you do now.

To be SEO effective you want your backlinks to leave great "footprints". Backlinks that leave great footprints are:

- **Natural** – Stay away from doing an enormous amount of backlinks at one given time like the 10,000 -50,000 ones that I referred to.
- **Consistent** – You have to consistently build backlinks to rank ahead of your competitors. Plus search engines love link building consistency.
- **Quality** – Make sure you build quality backlinks and remember a quality backlink is any backlink that helps your site improve its ranking in the search engines.
- **Varied** – You want backlinks from different sources. These multiple sources are covered next in the off page optimization factors.

Off-Page Optimization Factors

- **Article Writing and Submission** – This off page optimization factor I covered earlier. Article writing and submission is a great way to obtain quality backlinks and visitors to your site.

- **Social Bookmarking** — Social bookmarking allows people to share bookmarks to websites that they think would be of interest to others. In short, Social Bookmarking websites are sites that categorize and store 'bookmarks' just like you would add a site to your Favorites. Only in this case they are accessible to anyone on the internet.

  Millions of people visit social bookmarking sites every day looking for recommended sites. These sites get millions of visitors and are great for generating relevant traffic to your website as well as creating automatic backlinks that will enable your website to increase its ranking in the search engines.

- **Profile Creation** – You can obtain backlinks by creating profile links at various websites. So what is a profile link? Profile means a page that contains membership details, and a profile link is the direct anchor text link on the profile page that links to your site / page. Profile links are great for link building because your links are the only links on the page which gives you maximum link juice from the main domain of the site.

- **Blog Commenting** – Blog Commenting is the activity of posting feedback or comments in blog posts in order to get backlinks and referral traffic to your website. This doesn't mean that anyone can write anything in any blog, it means that comments on posts need to be relevant, thought provoking and intelligent.

- **Directory Submission** – Directory submission is the activity of adding your website to the various web directories on the internet in your niche's category with the purpose of increasing your site's visibility and obtaining backlinks.

- **Press Release Submission** – Not only are online press releases a great way for your online business to gain media exposure but they are also great for traffic, publicity, search engine visibility and getting backlinks.

To create an effective press release that will result into maximum exposure for your online business, you have to choose a strong press release topic that will pique people's interest. You also have to create a compelling headline that will attract eyeballs and the first sentence of the body of your press release called a lead should inspire your readers to keep reading.

- **Forum Posting** – Forum postings in your website's niche is a great way to connect to potential customers, drive traffic to your site and show your expertise. You can obtain backlinks through your "signature" which allows you to include your website's url and anchor text. When you participate in the forum discussions by answering or posing questions your signature is viewable below your forum post.

When you are writing your forum posts make sure they are well written and properly optimized with your keywords so that they can easily attract and get indexed by the search engines. This will benefit your site's ranking.

- **Social Media Optimization** – Social media optimization is an important factor in off-page optimization because it is another way that search engines value the importance of a website. We are living in a social media world and you or your business should have various social media profiles across the internet that are optimized with your main keywords with a direct link back to your website.

- **Video Submission** – Video submission is another one of those ways that you can dominate the search engines via another path when you fully optimize your video's title, keyword tags and description to include your main keywords as well as a link back to your website.

The search engines include videos from various video sites like YouTube in their rankings and since these sites have a high page rank and your video is considered content on their site it will receive instant exposure in the search engines. Some of my YouTube videos have received first page rankings on Google and as a result I receive a lot of traffic because my video's description contained a link back to my site and I also strategically mentioned it in the video.

Deep Linking

Since we are on the topic of off page optimization and backlinks it is essential that you know about deep linking. What is deep linking? A deep link is basically a backlink that is pointed towards a web page on your site, rather than the homepage itself. Here are examples of some deep links within my site.

Home Page

http://www.getseobacklinks.com

Deep Link

http://www.getseobacklinks.com/socialbookmarking.html

Deep Link

http://www.getseobacklinks.com/seoservices.html

Deep Link

http://www.getseobacklinks.com/articlewritingsubmission.ht ml

Deep Link

http://www.getseobacklinks.com/premiumbacklinks.html

Deep Link

http://www.getseobacklinks.com/blogcommentingservice.ht ml

As you notice the url of my deep links contain the keywords that are relevant to the content and what I am offering on a particular web page. For example the url http://www.getseobacklinks.com/blogcommentingservic e.html is the web page where I offer my blog commenting service. When you visit this particular url you will see that my title bar contains the keywords that are relevant to that page.

This is how my title bar reads:

Blog Commenting Service One Way Backlinks

This title along with the url, content and keywords are optimized for the search engines and this positions the web page to receive laser targeted organic search engine traffic when people type in the search query "Blog Commenting Service" , "Blog Commenting" or long tail keywords phrases associated with those keywords.

So to increase the search engine rankings for that particular web page I consistently create backlinks, but instead of those backlinks being directed towards my home page, they are directed towards the url http://www.getseobacklinks.com/blogcommentingservic e.html. The keyword anchor text that I currently use is Blog Commenting Service for maximum optimization.

When you are creating your Google Adwords pay per click campaigns make sure that your ads and the keywords that you choose for your campaigns are relevant to the content on the particular web page that you're sending traffic to when you're deep linking or sending traffic to your home page, because if it is not you will receive a low quality score from Google and your pay per click ad will be shown less frequently or not shown at all.

Crawling and Indexing

In order for your website to be included in the search engines, it must be crawled first and then indexed. Crawling is when search engine spiders visit a website and moves from web page to web page by following the links on those pages. The pages that are found are then ranked using an algorithm and indexed into the search engine's database.

So indexing is simply the process by which the content on your web page is examined and included into the "index" which is the search engine's database of keywords and associated pages (URL'S) containing them. To find out if your site has been indexed on Google, Yahoo or Bing just enter your site's name i.e. "yoursite.com", click the search button and the results will show how many times your site is referenced.

Since getting crawled is the first step in getting your web pages indexed by the search engines here is a list of crawling factors.

Crawling Factors

- **Internal link structure** – Your site has to have an internal link structure that makes it easy to crawl. Placing a sitemap on your website will further assist search engine spiders in finding all the content on your website.

- **Update your content often and regularly** – By updating your content the search engine spiders have a reason to visit and revisit your site because search engines love fresh new relevant content. When you have done an update on your site you can actually invite the search engine spiders to crawl it by sending out a Ping. A Ping lets them know that you have new content.

- **Backlinks** – Getting backlinks from regularly crawled sites will help your site get crawled and indexed quickly.

- **Page Loading Time** – Be sure to check your website's loading time because this can affect the search engine spider's ability to crawl your site.

You can use a free service by Google called Google Webmaster Tools which analyzes your website crawl errors, crawl statistics and offers HTML code suggestions to make your website more search engine friendly.

In wrapping up the crawling factors I must note that if you don't want certain pages on your website crawled you can add a robot.txt file which tells the search engines not to crawl that specific web page.

Now let's move on to discuss and debunk some of the common SEO myths that are out there so that you can separate truth from fiction.

SEO Myth #1

You Need To Submit Your Website To The Search Engines

There are plenty of companies out there that offer to submit your website to the search engines for a fee. This is totally unnecessary because the fact is inclusion in the search engines is free and as stated previously it happens by good on-page and off-page optimization that allow the search engine spiders to crawl and index your site.

SEO Myth #2

You Can SEO A Website Just Once

SEO is certainly not a one-time occurrence and you need to pay regular attention to your website because the variables to search rankings are always changing as the search engines tweak their algorithms and reassess how they view the level of importance of websites in relationship to each other. The Panda update by Google is a recent example of an algorithm change that affected many websites search engine rankings.

In addition, your competitors are constantly improving their website's optimization and are consistently building backlinks to increase their search engine rankings. So if you're not investing in SEO on a regular basis then you are falling behind.

SEO Myth #3

If You Have More Backlinks Than Your Competitors You Will Outrank Them

Although you should be relentlessly building backlinks to your site there is a misconception and an erroneous belief that if you have more backlinks than your competitors you will outrank them.

For example, if your main competition is at the #1 position on Google and they have 5,000 backlinks to their website for you to over- take them and occupy that number 1 position all you would have to do is get 5,001 backlinks and you will knock them out of the top ranking. This notion is ludicrous.

First of all, as you have learned already there are many variables that determine where a website will rank and backlinks are just one variable. In fact, Matt Cutts Google's go to guy mentioned at a conference that there are 200 variables that Google's uses to rank a site so that totally debunks this myth.

SEO Myth #4

NoFollow Backlinks Are Not Worth It Because They Have No Value

Before I tackle this myth let me explain to you what a nofollow link is. A no follow link is a way for webmasters to tell search engines not to follow any links on a page of their website or a specific link on their website. Conversely, a dofollow link is the complete opposite.

The no-follow attribute also tells the search engine that a website doesn't editorially vouch for the backlinks that are created on their site. This led to the false belief that nofollow links are not valuable. This is simply not true because the major search engines count all links nofollow and dofollow plus if a website had strictly nofollow backlinks this would look suspicious to the search engines and may result in the loss of rankings. So when you are creating backlinks for your site make sure you have a good ratio of nofollow and dofollow links because it looks natural to the search engines.

SEO Myth #5

A High Google Page Rank = High Ranking

Let's get this straight right now even though it's nice to have a high Google Page Rank it does not equal a high ranking. It's one of those prevalent SEO myths that got circulated some time ago. Based on my experience a low pr page can actually outrank a high pr page in the search engines. So don't get hung up on your website's page rank, just concern yourself with making sure that your website is search engine optimized.

SEO Myth #6

The Loading Time Of My Website Is Irrelevant

Think again. Search engines place a heavy emphasis on the user experience and if your website takes an inordinate amount of time to load then it negatively impacts your visitors. So the bottom line is, the faster your website loads the better the user experience and the greater the chance you have to rank for your keywords in the search engines.

SEO Myth #7

My Website Was Ranked In Google's Search Engine For My Main Keyword Now It's Not Even Listed In Their Search Results I Must Have Done Something Wrong

If you didn't make any crazy changes to your website that would affect its search rankings and you didn't get one of those 50,000 backlinks in one day packages that I mentioned earlier then you didn't do anything wrong, your site is more than likely experiencing what is referred to in SEO circles as the "Google Dance".

The "Google Dance" is the period when Google is rebuilding its rankings and the search engine results fluctuate for a short period of time. You may see your site go down in its rankings or you might not see it at all in Google's search engine until the update is completed. So don't worry you didn't do anything wrong. Every site experiences the "Google Dance".

SEO Myth #8

First Page Rankings Happen Overnight

Once in a blue moon this does happen but it is more a result of serendipity. So let me ask you when was the last time you saw a blue moon? Exactly. SEO takes work, experimentation, tweaking and patience to get first page rankings in the major search engines and this rarely happens overnight.

Plus there is a lot of competition for popular keywords. For example, for the keywords "make money online" there are 1.7 billion search results alone on Google and there are only 10 slots on the first page. You can achieve first page rankings for your keywords, but the bottom line is you will face competition. The key to overtaking your competitors is you have to know what you're doing in terms of an SEO and link building strategy or you must hire an SEO consultant or company to create and execute that strategy for you.

My company GetSeoBacklinks.com
(http://www.getseobacklinks.com) can assist you in your
quest for search engine domination. We not only offer a
superior SEO plan for your business, but we also give you
a superior backlinking copywriting strategy that will
enable your business to increase its search engine
rankings and sales conversions.

Our track record includes obtaining high search engine
rankings as well as first page rankings for our various
clients in every imaginable niche from A-Z.

Here's a brief run down on what you will receive when
you choose us to navigate your business to the first page
of Google, Yahoo and Bing:

Keyword Analysis

We will do a detailed keyword analysis of your website
and also give you a ranking report to show you exactly
where you currently stand on the 3 major search engines
top 100 positions for your website's existing keywords.

On-Page Optimization

We will point out the various ways in which you can
better optimize your website so that it is search engine
friendly.

Competitor Analysis

Competitor Analysis is the process of extensively researching your competitors. We would first make a list of your main competitors and analyze their sites using our state of the art software to decipher and decode the various techniques used by them.

We will also determine how many backlinks they have and where they are receiving those backlinks from. This will enable us to put together a comprehensive link building strategy for you.

SEO Copywriting Assistance

We analyze your website's copy and its SEO elements and make the necessary recommendations to you to ensure that your website is in the position to convert visitors into sales.

Off-Page Optimization (Link Building)

After determining the amount of backlinks your first page competitors have we will begin to gradually build quality premium backlinks to your website. Not only do we build quality premium backlinks to your site, but we get those backlinks indexed with our proprietary link indexing system. Why is the indexing of your backlinks important to your website's well-being? Because search engines don't count backlinks they can't see.

In fact, the majority of people who create backlinks suffer because on average only about 5% of their links ever get indexed! With us this <u>never happens</u>. If you want further information visit our website at GetSeobacklinks.com or **call us at (917) 406-3549**.

Your Search Engine Domination Mindset

To completely and utterly dominate the search engines you have to have the right mindset. What is a mindset? A mindset is universally defined as a habitual or characteristic mental attitude that determines how you will interpret and respond to situations. To put it even more simply, your mindset is your frame of mind.

To obtain your goal of high search engine rankings your mindset must be one of supreme confidence with the belief that you will be able to remain focus, committed and resilient enough to execute your strategy and achieve your goals no matter what the obstacles are.

Those obstacles could be that you're facing stiff competition for the keywords you want to rank high for, a sudden change in the search engine algorithms that results in a drop in your search rankings, something that is distracting you, or whatever the case may be. You must persevere! You must dominate! To dominate you have to have that killer instinct! If you presently don't have this kind of mindset it is because you have self-limiting beliefs that you need to completely annihilate if you want to succeed. Self-limiting beliefs are those things you believe about yourself that place limitations on your abilities. They may be conscious or unconscious. They may be founded or unfounded. For example:

I'm not a technical person so I won't be good at SEO I'm not a "lucky person" so I won't get to the first page of the search engines.

It may be true that you are not a technical person (whatever that means to you) but it doesn't mean you won't be good at SEO.In regards to you not being a "lucky person" let me make this perfectly clear to you, luck is not a criteria for getting on the first page of the search engines. The criteria is having an understanding of and executing all the variables that we discussed throughout this book that will enable you to position your site to garner first page rankings.

If you have self limiting beliefs and you need assistance in learning how to overcome them I offer an audio CD entitled "How To Overcome Your Self Limiting Beliefs". This amazing 41 minute audio CD will give you the blueprint that you need to overcome your self limiting beliefs forever. You can access it at the following link http://www.dominatingsearchengines.com/limiting.html

Make It Viral

In conclusion, I hope that by reading this book you have gained a basic and deeper understanding of SEO and how to effectively utilize it to dominate the search engines and turn your website into a cash generating juggernaut.

If this has been your experience, I would highly appreciate that you make this book viral by sharing it on Facebook, Twitter, Google+, by email etc. and telling friends, family, associates or anyone that you think might benefit from its contents.

Thanks,

Omar Johnson

Other Books By Author

How To Create A Profitable Ezine From Scratch

The Secrets Of Making $10,000 on Ebay in 30 Days

The Complete Guide To Investing in Gold And Silver: Surviving The Great Economic Depression

How To Sell Any Product Online:"Secrets of The Killer Sales Letter"

How To Make A Fortune Using The Public Domain

Creative Real Estate Investing Strategies And Tips

How to Make Money Online:"The Savvy Entrepreneur's Guide To Financial Freedom"

How to Overcome Your Self-Limiting Beliefs & Achieve Anything You Want

The Secrets of Finding The Perfect Ghostwriter For Your Book

The Creative Real Estate Marketing Equation: Motivated Sellers + Motivated Buyers = $

How To Start An Online Business With Less Than $200

How To Market Your Business Online and Offline

How To Promote Market And Sell Your Kindle Book

The Fine Art of Writing The Next Best Seller On Kindle

www.ingramcontent.com/pod-product-compliance
Lightning Source LLC
Chambersburg PA
CBHW071251170526
45165CB00003B/1305